# For The Love of Sports

# For The Love of Sports

First print edition.

Copyright © 2022 Mitchell Ryan Murtoff. All rights reserved.

Cover art © 2022  Mitchell Ryan Murtoff and Sarah Ickes.

ISBN: 979-8-9866350-0-2.

Library of Congress Control Number: 2022920861.



**Photography by:**

Sarah Ickes

Sky Strong

Lawrence Murtoff

Don Knoblet

**Edited by:**  Todd Coulson

# Table of Contents

# Acknowledgement

I would like to thank all my coaches from all of the different sports I played from the age of 6 until adulthood who helped mentor my love of each sport I played.  Along with instilling the love of each sport, I would also like to thank them for teaching me discipline, which transferred over to other areas of my life.  I would like to thank the following individuals who took time to coach me and the rest of my teammates and for instilling values in us that not only helped make us better athletes, but also better people.  There were many coaches along the way. I will try to name as many as I can remember.  Some of my coaches included:  Larry Kline, Ronnie Cline, Ron Hewitt, Jeff Taylor, Fred Hibbs, Robert Klokis, Richard Tate, Pam Hewitt, Skip Martin, Barry Starner, William Celio, and Stan Doyle. I apologize if I have missed anyone.  I would also like to thank Donald Knoblet for introducing me to football (soccer) and ice hockey.  Without his zest for these sports, I would have never attempted to play them.  I also need to thank my teammates throughout the years for making these times very memorable.  I also need to thank some of my former coworkers from Lowes on Brice Rd in Columbus, Ohio for allowing me to be a part several softball teams.  I would like to thank Jimmy Richards and Joe Turek for inviting me to play on their softball and bowling teams in Columbus, Ohio.  I would also like to thank James Arzadon for inviting me to be a part of his recreational football (soccer) team in Ohio and presenting me with an assistant coaching opportunity for a youth football (soccer) team in Pickerington, Ohio. I also would like to thank my parents for taking me to all the practices and traveling to my games.

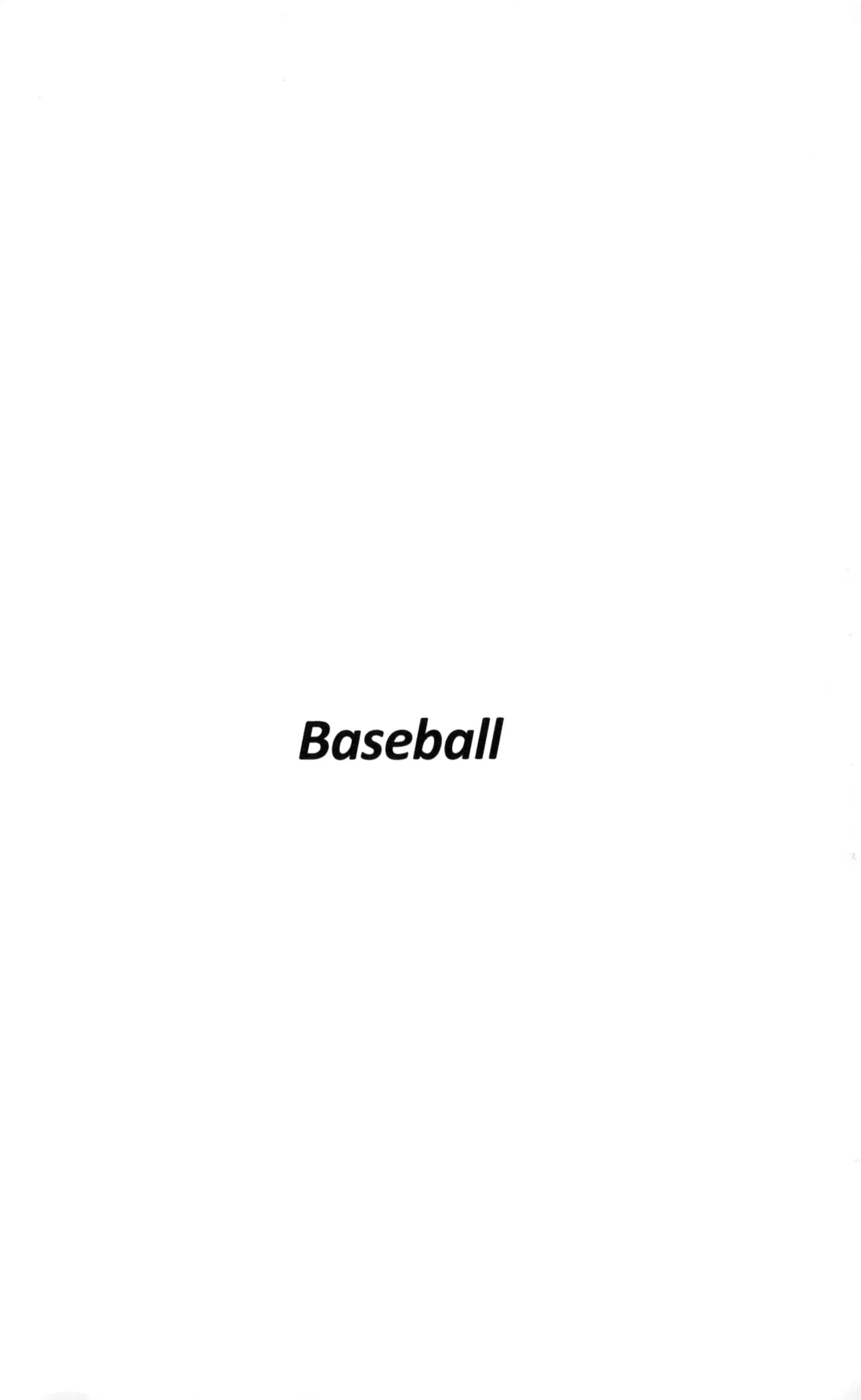

# Baseball

The days are now longer.  The temperature is rising.  It's summertime.  Which means it's time for the boys of summer.  The smell of the fresh cut grass in the outfield.  The chalk lines have been laid.  The umpire sweeps off home plate and yells "Batter up!"  The season is now underway.  The batter looks to the coach for a sign.  The pitcher checks with the catcher for a signal.  The batter steps into the batter's box looking to hit.  The pitcher winds up and hurls the ball towards home plate.  Swing and a miss!  The ball ends up in the catcher's mitt.  The umpire yells "Strike one!"  The batter steps out of the box and looks to the coach. Meanwhile, the pitcher looks to the catcher for the next sign.  The catcher signals for a curve ball.  The coach signals for the batter to take the pitch.  The chess match continues.  The batter steps into the box and prepares for the next pitch.  Low and away.  "Ball one!" yells the umpire.  The pitcher winds up and throws a fast ball.  He loses his grip on the ball and it sails on him and hits the batter.  The batter goes to first base after being checked for injuries.  Next batter up.  The runner takes a lead off first base.  The catcher sees this out of the corner of his eye.  The first baseman gets in position to hold the runner on the bag.  The catcher calls out a series of numbers for a play.  The runner takes a few extra steps towards second base. The pitcher goes into his windup and fires the ball towards home.  The batter swings and misses.  The catcher fakes a throw to the pitcher from his knees and rifles the ball to the first baseman.  The runner dives towards first base and is too late.  He has been picked off!

The pitcher throws to the batter and he hits the ball into the outfield.  He stops at first base with a single.  The first basemen stands at the ready.  The runner takes a lead while the next batter steps into the batter's box.  The pitcher looks over his shoulder and notices the runner has taken a rather large lead.  He opts to pitch from the stretch position.  The catcher gives the signal and the pitcher attempts to pick the runner off.  The runner takes off towards second base.  The first baseman catches the ball and fires it to second base.  The ball gets there before the runner.  He comes to a dead stop and runs back towards first.  The second baseman gives chase and then rifles the ball to the first baseman.  Meanwhile, the shortstop now runs towards second and the pitcher backs up first base.  The pitcher catches the ball and the runner once again changes direction.  He is now in a pickle.  The pitcher throws the ball to the shortstop.  They almost have him!  The runner dodges the tag and sprints back towards first base.  The catcher has now taken position at first base and catches the ball.  The runner slides back into first.  The catcher applies the tag and the umpire yells "You're out!"

The game progresses while the strategy intensifies.  The home team scores a few runs while the visitors also tally a few as well.  The game is now tied.   It's the bottom of the ninth.  Two outs.  Bases are loaded.  Top of the lineup.  This batter is very reliable.  He looks to the coach.  The coach goes through a series of signs to try and confuse the opposing team's coach.  The catcher gives the sign for a curve ball.  The pitcher nods.  Pitching from the stretch, he checks on the base runners and goes into his windup.  The ball heads towards home plate and then suddenly breaks low and away.  The batter watches.  "Ball one!" says the umpire.  The pitcher now tries a fast ball.  It catches the inside corner of home plate.  "Strike one!" exclaims the umpire.  The batter looks to the coach again.  He indicates to swing away.  The pitcher rocks back into his position.  The catcher signals for a knuckle ball; a risky call for the situation.  The pitcher hurls the ball towards home plate.  The batter sees the lack of rotation on it and tries to adjust his swing speed to it.  He swings too fast as the bottom drops out of it.  The ball squirts past the catcher.  The pitcher sprints towards home as the baserunner makes a mad dash for home.  The catcher flips the ball towards the pitcher as he blocks home plate.  The crowd is on their feet!  The runner starts to slide and goes around the pitcher.  He then reaches back across his body to slide his hand across home plate. The pitcher catches the ball and lunges towards the runner.  He swipes his glove across the runner's hand as he slides across home plate.  "Safe!" proclaims the umpire!  The crowd goes wild!  The field is rushed by the home team and several exuberant fans! They have beaten their dreaded rivals for the first time in eight years!  After the celebration, the coaches and players from opposing teams do the traditional handshake line.  While there is some animosity between the two teams, both coaching staffs instilled the value of respect for others in their players.

# *American Football*

There is a chill in the air.  Hoodies and bonfires are now part of the social scene.  The equipment has been handed out.  There have been many long hours of practice and film study.  Positions have been assigned.  Play calling has been changed and strategies have been formulated.  The lights have been turned on in the stadium.  It's game time!

The teams rush onto the field from opposing tunnels.  The fans go crazy! Both groups are cheering fervently to inspire their team.  The captains approach midfield to meet the officials.  They shake hands and prepare for the coin toss.  The home team will make the call.  They call heads.  The officials acknowledge the call and commence with the coin toss.  They flip the coin and it lands heads up.  The home team opts to defer the opening possession until the second half.

The home team kicks off while the return man for the away team waits for the ball.  He catches it cleanly and takes off with blinding speed.  He stops and changes direction to make the first would-be tackler miss.  He eludes the next two tacklers.  He is then leveled by the back- up linebacker who also plays on the kickoff team.  The pads crack and the collision sends the return man back a couple of yards with the tackler landing on him.  He staggers as he gets up to run off the field.  The heavy hits will continue all night from both teams as the bitter rivals engage in this heavyweight grudge match for the state championship.

The away team's offense takes the field. They have the top-rated quarterback in the state at the helm.  The home team's defense is led by an all-state safety. Let the chess match begin.  On the first play from scrimmage, the quarterback drops back to pass.  He's looking for his favorite receiver running a go route. The left defensive end does a devastating swim to breeze right by the tackle and then tosses the running back out of the way.  He slams the quarterback to the ground, helmet first, just as he releases the ball.  The ball comes up short as an incomplete pass.  The quarterback struggles to get up.  He manages to collect himself and call the next play.   The coach realizes he must help protect his star from the tremendous hits if they want to claim the title.  It's a running play.  The center snaps the ball.  The quarterback hands the ball off to the running back and he runs to the right of the center.  He slips through a tackle and reaches the secondary where he is greeted by the safety.  The tackle sounds like a thunderclap followed by a loud thud as they fall to the turf.  The runner is just short of the first down marker. The quarterback looks to the sideline. The coach calls the play.  The offense sets up in a running formation.  The defense lines up accordingly.  The center snaps the ball on 2.  The quarterback goes to hand the ball off.  The defense rushes in to fill the hole the running back is looking to go through.  The quarterback pulls the ball and throws it to his open receive for a first down.  The defense tightens up and stymies the drive, forcing the away team to punt.

The away team lines up in punt formation.  The long snapper sends the ball back to the punter and he hits a booming kick that sends the return man back 10 yards to field it.  He catches it cleanly and takes off like a rocket.  He heads toward the right side of the field behind his blockers.  He sidesteps one tackler.  He looks up in time to see a defender flying towards him at top speed.  He does a video game like spin move and leaves the defender grasping at the air.  He manages to make a few more men miss and sees a lane open for a straight shot to the endzone.  It's now a footrace.  He is out in front of everyone except the punter.  The punter comes running at the return man.  The return man sees him coming and with a mighty stiff arm to the face, he throws the punter to the side like a ragdoll.  The return man turns on the afterburners and races into the endzone for the first touchdown of the game.  The home team fans erupt with cheers!  They line up for the extra point and it's good!

On the ensuing drive, the away team's offense starts to click.  The coach has made some in game adjustments to his strategy.  They have completed two pass plays for a large chunk of yardage.  The coach opts to go up tempo to wear out the defense.  They call a running play which catches the defense off guard.  The running back gains 15 yards after weaving through the defenders.  It's his longest gain of the night so far.  The fans of the away team rise to their feet and cheer to encourage their team.  The next play, the quarterback fakes a handoff to the wide receiver who came in motion and drops back to pass.  He sees his receiver wide open behind the defense.  He unleashes a bomb that covers 50 yards!  The receiver catches it in stride over his shoulder and takes off at top speed.  No one can catch him!  Touchdown visitors!  The extra point is good; tie game going into halftime.

The second half gets underway.  The home team receives the opening kickoff.  The return man gains minimal yardage. The offense is ready to show what it can do.  Their coach also adjusted his play calling and overall strategy.  They run a quarterback draw right up the middle.  The linebacker stops him short of the first down.  A few more plays results in a punt.  The away team's offense takes the field looking to build on their success in the first half.  This time the defense blitzes almost every play to disrupt the timing of the quick passes.  The away team manages to complete a few passes and run for a few yards. They are forced to punt.

The two teams continue to exchange heavy blows with bone crushing hits on every tackle.  It has begun to take its toll on both sides.  Players are starting to get up slowly and wincing.  The third quarter ends in the same score.  Heading into the fourth quarter, the coaches continue with adjustments to try and gain an advantage.  The teams are locked in a stalemate.

The away team finally gets within field goal range.  They look to try a few plays to get in the endzone.  The coach calls a timeout as the clock begins to wind down.  They draw up a couple of new plays to try. The quarterback calls his teammates into the huddle and calls the play.  They line up and snap the ball.  The receiver comes right behind the offensive line and catches a shovel pass from the quarterback.  He takes off towards the right side of the field.  The defense begins to pursue him across the field.  They make a run at him.  He turns around and throws the ball back to the quarterback.  The quarterback catches and looks downfield.  He sees his favorite receiver close to the endzone. He launches it.  The safety had taken a few steps in but was prepared this time.  He recovers from the misstep and covers the distance quickly.  Both the receiver and the safety jump for the ball. The safety wrestles it away and hits the ground.  The ball comes out. Incomplete pass.  It almost cost them the game.  The coach goes conservative and calls a running play.  They have some success.  The quarterback calls another running play.  The defense steps up and stops the running back in his tracks.

The coach calls timeout with a few seconds remaining to get his field goal unit on the field. It's within the kicker's range. They line up. The defense gets set. The long snapper hikes the ball. The safety jumps over the offense line and makes a mad dash towards the kicker. He blocks with one hand. The ball is loose on the ground. The clock is now at 0:00. The linebacker comes surging through and scoops up the ball. He charges down the field. He has a lot of real estate to cover to score the game winning touchdown. The home team fans rise to their feet and cheer him on! He runs as fast as he can. A defender catches up to him and tries to wrestle him to the ground. He sheds him fairly easily. 50 yards to go. A couple of other players get close. He turns it up a notch and accelerates. The safety gets to his feet and tries to catch to his teammate to help ward off would-be tacklers. 40 yards to go. The whole field goal unit has given chase. The other defenders have also started pursuing. 30 yards to go. Another player tries to tackle the linebacker. He manages to slow him up. A second tackler catches up and grabs him by the arm. He struggles to maintain his balance. One of them slip off and the other is starting to lose his grip as well. 20 yards to go. The safety and other teammates are doing their best to block all would be tacklers. The linebacker is growing weary. Another would-be tackler slips the defense and swats at the ball. He almost fumbles. He regains control of the ball and continues to run. 10 yards to go. The fastest players from the field goal unit have caught up to him. One jumps on his back and tries to punch the ball free. The linebacker is stout and carries him while another tackler goes for his legs. He is only able to hold onto one leg. The linebacker is now dragging his leg plus carrying the other player who has a firm grip on his shoulder pads. He is struggling mightily with the two players latching onto him. 5 yards to go. He sees the goal line is within reach. A third player is now attempting to knock the ball free. He summons all his strength and adrenaline to make the final push. The safety comes charging into the group to help push the struggling linebacker into the endzone. 2 yards to go. The safety continues to drive his legs to keep the pile moving. 1 yard to go. The linebacker begins to stumble and falls towards the goal line. He leans forward with the safety pushing as hard as can. He stretches as far as he can. He lands on the ground in a heap with the other players landing on top of him. The officials come racing in to check the spot of the ball. They pull the players off the linebacker to see. He has barely broken the plane of the endzone.  The referees signal touchdown!  The home team wins the state championship!  The players and fans storm the field!  It's pandemonium!  It's their first ever state title!  Fans begin to climb the goalpost and start to shake it.  It comes crashing down!  The whole town celebrates for the next several weeks.

# Basketball

The gym is packed for one of the most anticipated matchups of the season.  The number one ranked team against the number two ranked team in the district.  Both teams are undefeated.  The local media has hyped the game for the past few weeks and the powerhouses are now set to collide for the top spot in the district.

The opposing teams enter from opposite ends of the gym.  The fans jump to their feet.  The players begin to warm up, trying to stay focused on their routine while still sneaking a few peeks at their opponent.  The coaches have been preparing game plans and studying film on player tendencies for weeks.  This game will determine playoff seeding.  Some of the players have been talking smack in the local media outlets which has added to the intensity of tonight.

The players continue warming up while the coaches meet at center court to shake hands and meet with the referees for tonight's game. One of the stars from the visiting team starts to talk trash to the home team captain.  The two get very close to each other and continue the conversation.  Other players join in the huddle.  A couple of them start shoving each other.  The referees and coaches quickly break up the melee.  The head official issues a stern warning to each team and head coach that taunting will not be tolerated and players could face ejection if it continues.

Play resumes. Both teams score at a frantic pace. Up and down the court all the players go, transitioning from offense to defense seamlessly. The visiting team tries to slow the pace of the game by running set plays. They pass the ball inside to their center and let him go to work in the trenches. He starts to back down the home team's center and scores with a hook shot. The home team inbounds the ball and tries to push the issue with an up-tempo offense. The point guard zips a lightning quick pass to the small forward who slashed across the lane and hits a quick turnaround jumper. The visiting team brings the ball back down court and sets up for another set play. Once again, the point guard passes the ball into the center. He starts to back down the home team's center and is getting ready to shoot, when the home team's small forward dashed in from the perimeter and swats the ball out of the center's hands. He starts to dribble the ball up court and checks the clock. There are thirty seconds left in the half. He thinks about calling a timeout to regroup and run a set play but decided against it.

The small forward sets up at the top of the key and waits for everyone to get ready. He dribbles and waits for the clock to reach ten seconds then he makes his move. He does a crossover dribble and his defender falls on the floor and goes gliding out of the way. He takes a quick first step to get past him before he can recover. The center and power forward both step in the way to prevent him from scoring. He spots the shooting guard spotting up behind the three-point line and passes a laser quick pass to him. He catches the ball and shoots right away. Swish! Nothing but the bottom of the net! The horn sounds for the end of the second quarter. The home team is up by three points. Both teams head to their locker rooms to discuss strategies for the second half.

Both teams make their way onto the court for the start of the third quarter. There is a brief warm up period and once again players from both teams begin talking trash. The officials give a brief but effective warning to the players involved. The teams continue to warm up without further incident.

The third quarter starts with both teams slowing down the pace and being methodical. They were both going for high percentage shots. The teams continued to exchange baskets for most of the third quarter. Then, the visiting team caught a break. The home team had missed a shot and their small forward grabbed the rebound. He saw their point guard flying down the court and he whipped a baseball pass to him. He caught it and scored all in one motion. The visiting team was now only down by one point. The home team began to struggle and missed several shots. The opposing team capitalized on these opportunities and scored on the next eight possessions. They finished the third quarter by going on a sixteen-point run, putting them in control of the game. A few of them started trash talking again, but their coach reeled them in and stopped them before the officials could get there.

The home team's coach decided to change strategies. He told his players to go up-tempo again. He noticed some of the players on the opposing side were getting a little winded. Both teams broke their huddles and headed back onto the court. The home team started the fourth quarter with the ball. They wasted no time in turning up the pace of the game. They ran down the court and caught the opposing team by surprise. They scored an easy basket. The coach yelled out a play call. The team responded with a full court press defense. This caused all kinds of confusion and frustration for the visiting team. They even had a difficult time getting the ball inbounds, let alone past center court. The guards from the home team pinned their ears back and started to steal the ball on several straight possessions. They had cut the lead to three points. The visitors' coach called for a timeout. He was not happy with how his team had responded to the pressure. He instructed them to slow the pace down again. He could see fatigue setting in on his players. He asked for a full timeout to give them a chance to catch their breath.

After the timeout, both teams returned to the court. The visiting team was still a little winded. There was about five minutes left in the game. It was still up for grabs. The visitors had the ball following the timeout. They began implementing their new strategy and tried to impose their will on the home team. They let the center go to work for a few plays and he scored several baskets. The home team responded with more up-tempo basketball. They were keeping pace with the visitors, barely clinging to their one-point lead.

The next trip down the court saw the opposing team give the ball to their power forward. He posted up the small forward and did a quick spin move to get around him and dunked on him. The small forward tried to block the shot but fouled him. This sent the power forward to the free throw line. He had struggled all season at the line, but this time he came through. The game was now tied with two minutes to go. The home teams' coach called a timeout. He wanted to settle his team down and to also give them a breather for the final stretch of the game. He outlined the strategy for the rest of the game and then requested the timeout be changed to a full timeout. He decided to give a quick pep talk to his team.

"Guys, your season and legacy are on the line. You have fought so hard this season and come to far not to win the championship. I believe in each and every one of you. Believe and trust in each other. You are the most talented team I have ever coached. You will go down in school history when we win this game. Now get out there and play your hearts out! You will win! Now get out there and prove me right and make all of us proud!"

The horn sounded for the end of the timeout. The coach called everyone in for quick huddle for one last pump of adrenaline and sent them back onto the court. The home team had the ball coming out of the timeout. The coach still wanted an up-tempo pace to continue to wear down the opposition. The team pulled together like never before and began to dominate the other team. They scored four straight baskets to take a commanding lead with just one minute left in the game. The visiting team called a timeout. Their coach instructed them to pick up the pace and start a full court press. He also sent a couple of taller players from the bench into the game to help slow down the game hoping for some easy turnovers. His strategy worked. The backup players came through and scored easy buckets off turnovers to tie the game. The home coach called another timeout to slow down the game. He urged his guys to finish out the game. There was now only thirty seconds left in the game. The teams went back out onto the court. The home team had the ball. The center inbounded the ball to the small forward. The power forward for the opposing team charged and knocked him over. This resulted in a flagrant foul. The home team's coach was livid.

The small forward managed to pick himself up off the court but was slightly dazed. He had to shoot two free throws. He shot the first one and missed. He needed to make the next one to seal the game. There was only fifteen seconds left in the game. The visiting team called a thirty second timeout to discuss strategy. Everyone lined up for the second free throw and got ready. He took the shot and missed. It was a long rebound and the opposing team grabbed it. Their power forward was fouled immediately to stop the clock. There were ten seconds left in the game. It was a two-shot foul.

Everyone lined up for the first one. He bounced the ball a couple times to get into a rhythm and took the shot. He missed. The game was still tied. He walked away from the line and shook his head. Both teams were out of timeouts. He gathered himself to prepare for the next shot. He stepped up to the free throw line and was given the ball by the official. He took a couple of dribbles and was ready to shoot. The ball left his hands and he missed. The ball clanked off the side of the rim and almost went out of bounds. The point guard, of all people, scooped up the rebound and sprinted towards the other end of the court. The small forward had a head start on him. He was almost to midcourt when both guards from the opposing team formed a wall and jumped to prevent him from shooting. He jumped, did a 180 spin, and launched the ball over top of them to the other end of the court. The small forward caught the ball in stride, took one step, and hit a three-pointer fading out of bounds just as the horn sounded! The home team won the state championship! Fans rushed the court and began to celebrate with their team.

# *Football*

# *(Soccer)*

The Faith Chapel Football Club also known as FCFC was started by my friend, Don Knoblet and me in the early nineties. The team was comprised of several church members and some of Don's friends. It started out with Don, Ben (Don's younger brother), Don's friend Mike (also known as The Idiot), and me. We would go to different schools in the area to practice and play. We would work on ball control drills, passing, shooting on goal, and just to have fun. A few other people would occasionally join us. I really had never played soccer before, whereas Don had played for several years in school. I started out playing defense along with Ben. Don was our forward. Mike was the goalie. I wore number 10. It was my old number from playing sports before and was also the number worn by most of the star players on soccer teams. One of my favorite players at the time was Marco Etcheverry from D.C. United of MLS.

Our practices were a lot of fun. All of us were improving at a fast pace. I developed great touch and could take some wicked shots on goal. One night we were practicing at Bermudian Springs High School. After warmups, we started to take shots on goal. Mike had been getting on our nerves really badly of late. He kept taking frequent smoke breaks and would hold up practice. Don and I were talking while others were shooting on goal. He said, "How about we make a bet?" I said OK and asked what the wager was. He said the first one to hit Mike in the face while taking a shot on goal would win a dinner at Applebee's.  It was just between Don and me. This became known as the Applebee's rule. It went into effect immediately. Don let a shot rip. It went into opposite corner of the net. I lofted three shots right over Mike's outstretched hand. We kept shooting and kept missing. Don took another shot and it was fairly close. It was my turn and I put everything I had into it and zipped a shot right passed his left ear. The ball had bent at the last second right in front of his face. Mike was terrified. Don, Ben, and I laughed hysterically for a few minutes. I couldn't believe I missed.

Another evening while we were practicing at Lamberton Middle School in Carlisle, PA, a large group of people approached us and began to kick a ball around on the opposite side of the field we were on. The ball got away from us and Don chased it down near the group. Don began talking with them. It turns out they were a large family that had relocated to the area from Pakistan. They started to come to the field for family gatherings and to play football. During the conversation, they had challenged us to a game. Don made all the arrangements with them. By now, we had enough players attending regularly to start playing games. This would be our first match. We met a few more times to practice before the match.

The day of the match finally arrived. We rolled into the parking lot of the school and began to warm up. The family from Pakistan arrived shortly after us. Some of our teammates were a little bit late, but they still made it. We did not have a referee, so we played on the honor system. The match started tentatively. Both teams were trying to feel each other out. After a few minutes, the Pakistani family organized an attack. They were very organized and had apparently played most of their lives. A few quick passes and boom! They scored a goal. We continued the match and struggled to get the ball into their half of the field. There were a few missed opportunities for our team in the first half. Their midfielders would dispossess us several times and transition to offense before our defense could recover. This resulted in several easy goals. At halftime, the score was 6-0, them. We were exhausted. They had run us all over the field.

We caught our breath during halftime and hydrated. We began to talk about a new strategy. Don decided it was time to change things up. He had me move to the wing position and put someone else back on defense to take my place. Some other changes were made to the lineup and we were ready for the second half.

The second half started with some success. We were able to possess the ball more and start to do set pieces. The scoring opportunities started going in our favor. Playing on the wing is probably my natural position because I have good vision for the field and can analyze situations and make quick decisions. I picked off one of their passes and started to press forward. I saw a lane open up; Don also saw it and made a run. I lofted the ball over the defense and he headed into the back of the net. We finally scored. It was close to the halfway point of the second half when we did.

They did not hesitate to score again. They scored on their next possession. They were able to pick off several passes and dissect our defense fairly easily. They scored a few more goals after that while we continued to struggle. The game was finally over. The score was 11-1. We were clearly outmatched, but we didn't let this discourage us.

We practiced even harder over the next few weeks. We started adding more set plays with different combinations of people to increase our chances of success. It was still a little difficult because not everyone would attend our practices. We had been practicing for several weeks when Don told us he had scheduled another match for us. This time it would be against another local church. The game was scheduled to be played at South Middleton Township Park in Boiling Springs, PA. We had a few more players this time. Some members of the church had actually shown up to cheer us on.

The match was about to begin. We felt really good about our chances this time. We were better prepared and in better shape. We shook hands before the kickoff. The match started off at a furious pace. The opposing team didn't waste any time in testing our defense. We were able to hold them off for most of the first half. Then, they slipped a quick pass through the defense and scored. We tried to counter but didn't score before the half ended.

We had a team meeting and encouraged each other to keep fighting. The scoring chances would come. We were still in the game. We had improved so much and the score reflected that. We decided to start running more set plays and to counter whenever possible.

The second half started. We had possession to start. We kept working the ball around the perimeter of the defense until I saw Don making a run. I ripped a quick pass and he put it in the back of the net. Our hard work and patience had paid off. We were on the score board and looking for more.

On their next possession they made several passes to break down the defense and scored again. On our next possession, we tried for a quick strike. We caught them on their heels. I sent quick pass to Don and he then made a fast-paced pass to his brother-in-law, Tim. Tim faked out the goalie and was getting ready to shoot. He had a wide-open net. He was within five feet of the net. He wound up and struck the ball. Somehow, the ball went almost completely vertical over the net. We were all dumbfounded. It looked like he somehow defied the laws of physics.

The other team scored again on the next possession. This made the score 3-1 them. It was time to rally the troops. I decided to join in on our attacks. I figured having an extra man close to the box would benefit us. I got the ball off the restart and began to press forward. I saw Ben in an open space and passed him the ball. I then took off like I was shot out of a cannon. I made a B-line for the goal. Ben saw this and passed the ball back to me. It was a little bit ahead of me. The goalie came off his line to try and stop me. I lunged at the ball at the last minute and barely touched it to send it underneath him in the near post. We were now within striking distance.

Both teams fought valiantly for the rest of the game. They had more scoring opportunities than us but Mike kept them out of the net. Their goalie did a phenomenal job against us the rest of the match. It was the end of the match. The score was 3-2, them. We shook hands with them and had a brief meeting. We were extremely happy with our performance. We had made great strides as a team. We were disappointed we didn't win, but still we saw a major improvement.

It was now the end of summer. Our church had its annual summer picnic. Everyone had eaten dinner and was talking. I was talking with one of the women that went there. She was single and was very nice. I was then summoned to play a game of football. We picked teams and began to play. This was just for fun. The teams were evenly matched. During the game, I was playing on the wing again and would join in on the attacks. Don's dad, the pastor, was playing defense. We were on the same team. He had intercepted an errant pass from the other team. I saw this and started to come towards him to receive the pass. He ripped a shot at me as hard as he could. The pace he struck it with caught me off guard. I tried to stop the ball with my knee to get it to drop to the ground. The ball tailed a little bit and struck me right in the groin. I dropped to the ground immediately, writhing in pain. I had to crawl several yards before I could get to my feet. The woman I had been talking with earlier saw this, got up and left. After the game, Don said his dad said this was to keep me from making a mistake. I muttered a few curse words and walked away. Don just laughed. This was the end of our soccer team. Most of the younger players were going back to school or college. The rest of the older people on the team decided not to play anymore after that summer.

# Volleyball

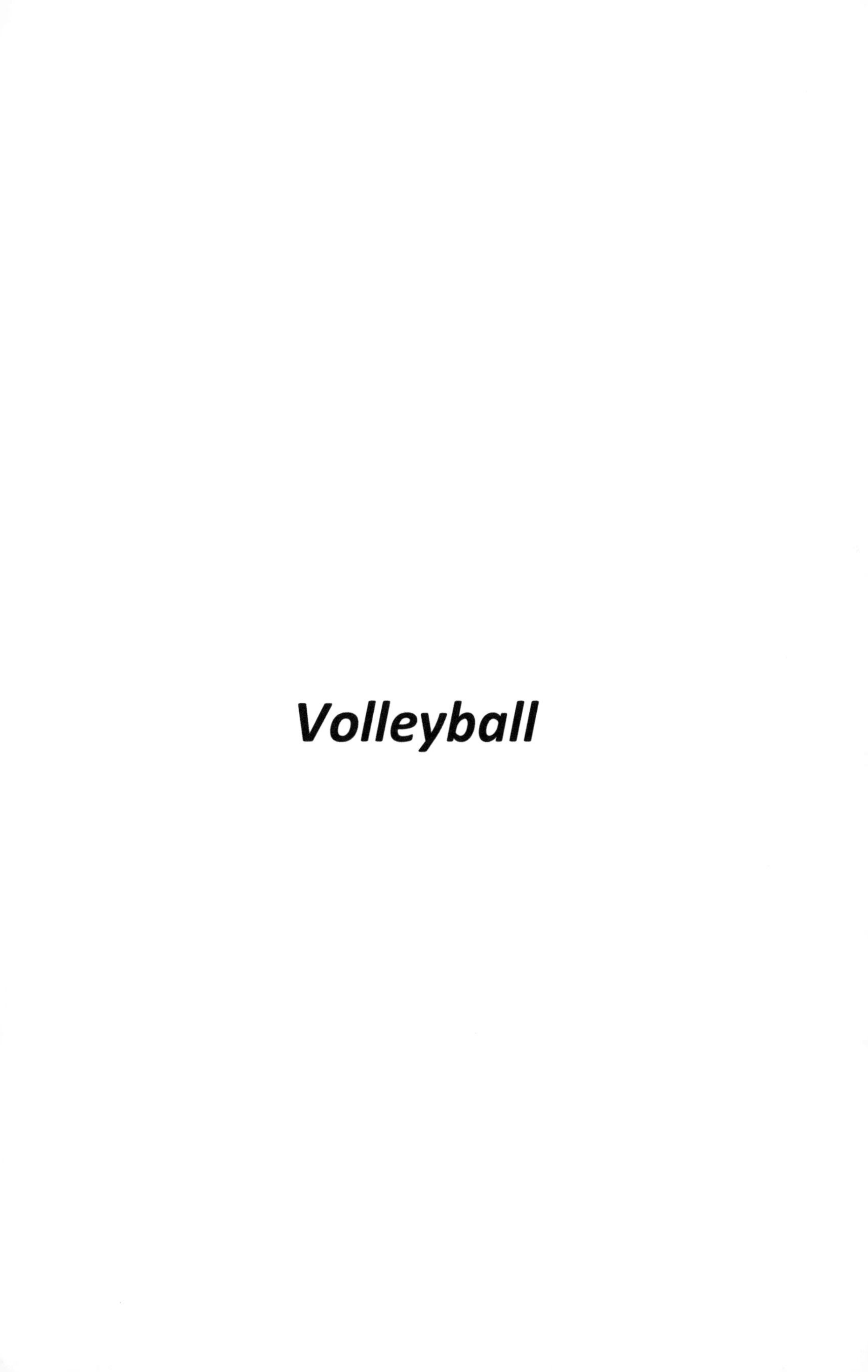

During my senior year in high school, I really got into volleyball. I was into it so much that I had my dad dig holes in the back yard to cement posts for a net. I really wanted to have it excavated and filled with sand, but that cost too much money for my family. I would have friends over to play a few times a week during the summer. Some evenings after work, I would practice my serve for hours at a time. I could hit all six position numbers on the court at any given time. I would just choose a spot and aim for it. I was deadly accurate.

In the fall I began my collegiate years at Elizabethtown College. I lived on campus. This was my first time living away from home. I found out that they had a men's volleyball team. I thought I would give it a shot. One Saturday they had a fair on campus for all the sports teams and clubs at the college. I found the volleyball team booth and signed up for tryouts. The captain asked if I had any playing experience. I told him I did not but still want to try out for the team. He said OK and said he would be contacting me once they arranged time for the tryouts.

There were sand courts on campus and I found myself there most weekends. I met a few other guys that were going to try out for the team as well. We became close friends and began to meet there whenever we could to practice. We would play for hours and then get together for a few drinks. Most of the guys there were better than me because they were from New Jersey and grew up playing beach volleyball. I worked hard and pretty soon I was just as good as them.

The day finally came for tryouts. I made sure I had plenty of rest the night before. I went to the gym and saw some of the guys were already there warming up. The captain got everyone's attention and we did quick introductions and got things started. He divided us up into teams. The upperclassmen versus the freshmen and a few other people new to the team. Despite not playing together, we did pretty good against them. My serves were to be reckoned with. I made a few of them look foolish. My passing needed some work during the game and I did get a few spikes to land inbounds. The tryouts were over after a few games. The captain told us he would call us in a few days to let us know if we made the team or not.

At the end of the following week, the phone in my dorm room rang. My roommate answered it and told me it was for me. I answered nervously and it was the volleyball team captain. He told me I had made the team. He told me that I would be playing mostly back row and sometimes second setter. I said thank you and hung up. I was super excited. Our season would officially begin in the spring semester. I picked number 10 since it was available.

The season started and we began with a bang. We won our first three matches. Then we faced Susquehanna University. They beat us badly. After that, we worked even harder than before. We had extra practices to prepare for our archrivals, Messiah College. There was a lot of bad blood between the two schools in every sport. Beating them would highlight of our season before the end of season tournament.

The match was a home game for us. We were psyched up for this. There was a large crowd cheering us on, like there always was when we would play Messiah. I was in the starting lineup for the game. The captain had me start off serving. It felt great to have his and the rest of the team's confidence in me, considering I was a walk on.

The first game was ready to start. They had the first serve. They scored a few points right away. They ran a very complex offense. It caught us off-guard at first. Then our blockers figured out one of their plays and shut them down. It was now my turn to serve. I caught the ball and took a few deep breaths. I bounced the ball three times like I always did before every serve. I tossed the ball and struck as hard as I could. Their back row player shanked the pass. This really helped settle me down. I ripped off another serve and this time they were ready and made a good pass. They ran a play but our front center player blocked the spike attempt. I got the ball again and followed my routine. This time I hit a light lofting serve that just barely cleared the net. It hit off their front row player's shoe after he misjudged it. This got us back in the game. On my next serve, they blocked our hitter's spike. I had done my part to start the game off for us. Now it was time to play defense.

They went on a run, ripping off five points before we stopped them. We responded by going on a run of our own. We got within two points of them and then hit a wall. We started shanking passes, missing blocks, and hitting errant spikes. They won the first game 21-10. We were somewhat embarrassed and the captain called a quick meeting to rally us. He said that was our bad game. We got it out of our systems.

The referee signaled for the next game to start. This time we had service first. I started the second game serving again. I was a little more warmed up this time and the adrenaline had subsided some. I felt more in control of myself and more relaxed. This time I started off with a soft serve just over the net at the opposite front corner. It hit just on the line as their player barely missed it. On my next serve, I hit a hard deep serve and it landed on the back line as their back row players watched it go by. Next, I dropped a lollipop serve in the center of their side of the court. A couple of their guys ran into each other because they didn't call it. This also dropped for an ace. I ripped off another serve, this time at the back corner on the same side of the court as I was on. Their player shanked it. I was really in a groove. I hit another rocket shot towards the back center of the court. This time, they were able to return it and score a point.

The rest of the game went back and forth with both teams making incredible plays on defense. Our blockers were figuring out their offense. Sometimes they would run decoy hitters to throw off the timing of our blockers. People were diving across the floor trying to save every point. Each team looked to capitalize on the other's mistakes. Things were really getting intense. The officials warned the captains about some of the guys talking trash or he would start ejecting people. We called a timeout and discussed this along with our strategy for the rest of the game. We ended up winning the second game 21-19.

The third game started and was even more intense. We would score several points, then they would go on a run and take the lead. They started to substitute their players more often to try to get them an advantage. It worked. They wiped the floor with us in the third game. The score was 21-9. We were getting tired and took some extra time to catch our breath and drink water and Gatorade to get us through the next game. Our matches were always the best of five. We had to win the next game to keep it going. We did a quick rally to help psych us back up again and were ready to go.

The fourth game started with them jumping out to an early lead. They were up 7-0 when our captain called a timeout. He said we really needed to dig deep and focus. This helped to slow down their momentum and give us a breather. It was my turn to serve. The captain looked at me and gave me the thumbs up. I was getting tired because I had been running all the court, diving after balls and scraping my knees on the gym floor. I would not let my team down. I started with my routine and served another ace. I kept it up and scored six more points, tying the game. I was picking them apart and making them look bad. On my next serve, they got a spike past our blockers. I had done my part and got us back in the game.

The game continued at a frantic pace. We exchanged points three or four at a time. The other guys were also doing well with their serves. The team was playing our best game of the day so far. We were not going to give up. We knew how important this game was. Our hitters came through with several big hits. Our middle hitter hit a thunderous spike inside the ten-foot line. This was our rallying cry as we won the fourth game 21-19.

The match was tied. It all came down to the fifth and final game for bragging rights. The referee gave us an extended break as both teams were exhausted. It was extra hot and humid in the gym that day. Our captain called us together for another quick meeting. He told us we had them on the ropes. They thought they could come into our house and wipe the floor with us. They had beaten our team in the past two seasons, handily. We had a few seniors on the team including the captain. They wanted to win this match really badly. All of us freshmen had made an immediate impact on the team. We did a big cheer to get ready for the final game of the match.

The fifth game was ready to be played. We kept our starting lineup the same since things were firing on all cylinders. I started off serving again. I got us five quick points before they got a side out. They went on another run and tied the game. This time our outside hitter ripped a shot across the court and hit the line to stop them. We scored two points before they stopped us from scoring again. They were looking to get into their offense with all the misdirection. Their back row player did a perfect pass to their setter. They sent a decoy hitter with another hitter right behind him. This time I was ready. I watched the decoy fly out of the way and lined up the hitter as he struck the ball. The ball changed direction and I had to dive to get the ball up. I just barely got it with one hand and could feel my skin burning on the floor. The ball made it to the setter and he set our middle hitter for a quick attack. He put it inside the ten-foot line again. The game was tied again.

One of our other back row players scored a few more points. Then, they scored four more points. They were up and our captain called a timeout. We were getting tired again and needed a breather. We gathered ourselves and went back on the court. They were up by two at this point. It was my turn to serve again. I dropped a serve right on the setter's head and it hit the ground before anyone could touch it. I reached back and hit the ball as hard as I could. I put some backspin on it. It was heading out of bounds but then dropped at the last second and just hit the line. I had tied the game up. I picked out the ten-foot line on the opposite side of the court from where I was. I hit the ball, putting a sideways spin on it. Everyone watched as the ball sliced to the left across the net and hit the sideline at the ten-foot line. This caused the other team to call a timeout. They were baffled by what I had just done.

The timeout was over but had given us a quick breather. I served two more times and we scored each time due to some tremendous hits from our outside hitters. We were going on a run. We scored again before they blocked one of our hitters. They served and ran their offense and caught us off guard by using two hitters but having the first hitter attack. They scored a few more points. The game was now tied again, 18-18. We went through an entire rotation without scoring any points. It was my time turn to serve again. I hit a rocket across the net. They were able to return it. They sent a lob over top of our blockers and I ran and dove into the bench to save the ball. I hit it back into play and ran back onto the court. We did a free ball to keep the rally going. Their outside hitter wound up and hit the ball out of bounds; 19-18. I tried another short serve and it worked. The constant change in speed and location was paying off again. Their outside hitter shanked the ball; 20-18. They called another timeout to ice me. I walked away from everyone as I was in a zone. My teammates understood. The referee blew his whistle and we went back onto the court. I did my routine and ripped a shot between the center back row and outside players. They both dove for it and got it up to the setter. The setter tried to do a quick middle attack but all our front-line players formed a wall and blocked him. The ball hit the floor. We won the game 21-20! We had beaten our archrivals. Our fans rushed the gym floor and we began to celebrate. After they cleared the floor, we shook hands with them. We didn't like each other at all but there was mutual respect.

Everyone Can Spank It,
But Can You Get It In?

Everyone Can Spank It,
But Can You Get It In?

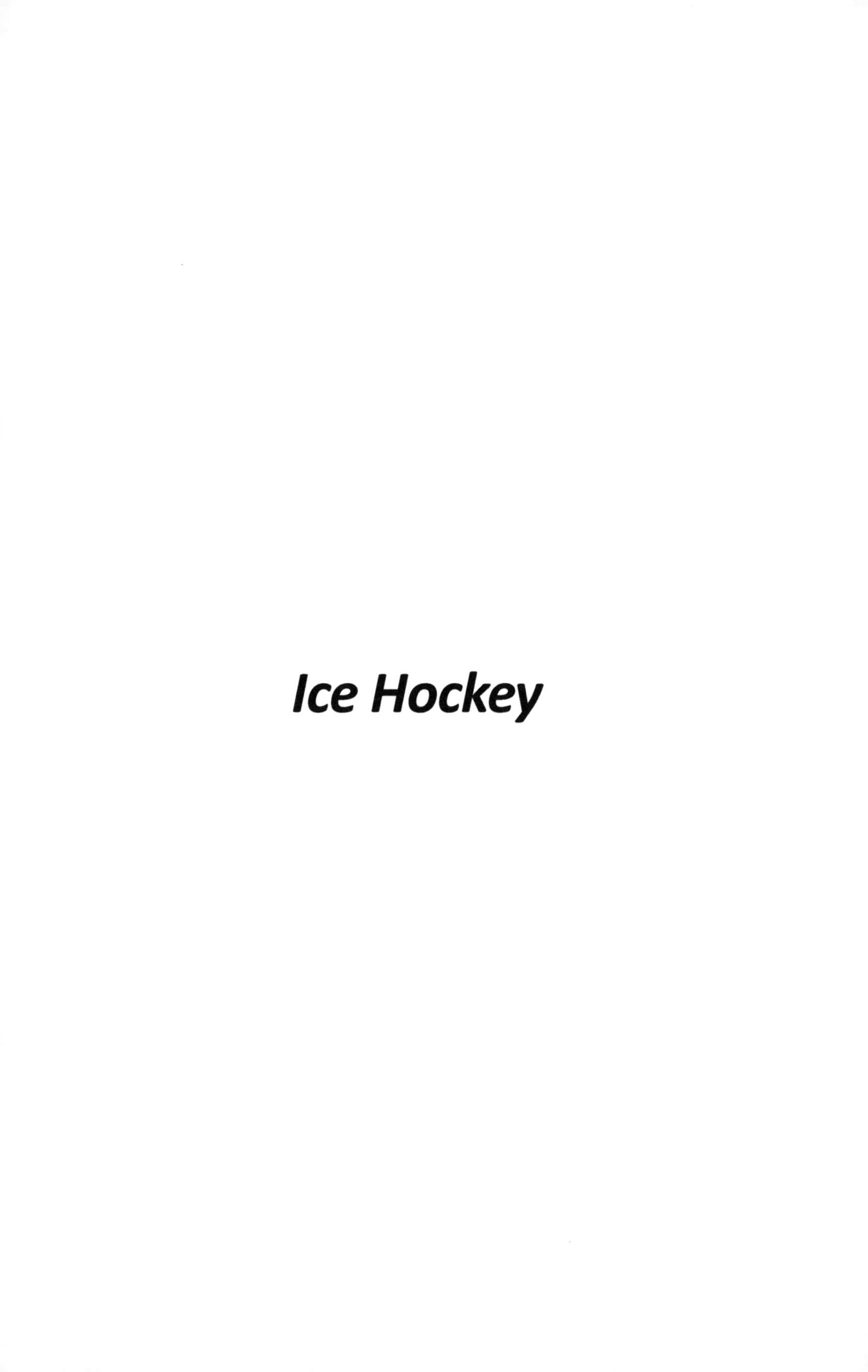

# Ice Hockey

I really didn't get into hockey until the mid-late 1990s. I began going to the Hershey Bears games and even attended a few Washington Capitals games. I even attended some Blue Jackets games once I lived in Columbus, but I did not start skating until 2001 when I lived in Reynoldsburg, Ohio. Don Knoblet and I were roommates at the time. His brother Ben was visiting from West Virginia. They had found a pond on the 18th hole of the Blacklick golf course and shoveled it off. They played against each other for a few days while Ben was visiting. Ben left and went back to West Virginia but forgot his skates. Don talked me into going to the pond and trying to skate. Ben's skates were three sizes too big for me which made me very clumsy at first. Don encouraged me to keep trying. I finally mustered the courage to get on the ice. I stood on the ice without falling right away. He gave me a few pointers and I picked it up easily. I started skating and picked up a lot of speed for my first time trying to skate. Unfortunately, I did not know how to stop. I crashed face first into the snowbank on the other side of the pond. Don laughed for several minutes but I did not let this deter me. I got back on the ice and started skating again. This time I took Ben's hockey stick with me and began to skate with it. Don and I worked on passing the puck back and forth to start with then while we were skating. I also picked up on this quickly. About fifteen to twenty minutes after I first stepped onto the ice, Don and I started playing one on one hockey. Surprisingly, I held my own against him. We each were scoring at a frantic pace. I always crashed into the snowbanks after I scored. We played for several hours. I think he scored a few more goals than me, but he told me I was really good for my first time ever playing hockey. I was hooked. I hadn't been this passionate about a sport since football (soccer).

There were several ice rinks in the area. My favorite ones were only about 20 minutes away from our townhome. I would go up to The Chiller at Easton and Nationwide Arena, the rink for the Columbus Blue Jackets. They have a practice rink that opens to the public for skating during certain hours. I would go several times a week and practice until I was extremely fast. It took me over a year to get really good. I bought a pair of hockey skates with my income tax refund and started using those instead of the rental skates at the rinks. I made several friends at The Chiller from going so often. I took a couple of my friends there to teach them how to skate. One of my friends, Jen, stuck with it for some time. She could get a few laps around the rink by herself. Another friend, Cary, on the other hand, struggled and quit after ten minutes. She would flip me off after she got off the ice every lap I did. I also took my ex-girlfriend to OhioHealth Ice Haus, the Blue Jackets practice rink, one time and she did really well.

After skating for a few years, I decided to buy all the gear for playing. I was excited about playing. There were Rec leagues at Easton for all skill levels. My goal was to join a league. I was always getting complimented about my skating, especially my speed and control. I could slow down but still couldn't stop or skate backwards. I found out they had drop-in hockey a couple days a week. I started going on my days off. It was kind of tough because I didn't know anyone. Most of the guys had been playing for years and probably played on a team together.

Since I was the new guy, they all tried to test me. I was mostly playing defense but would join in on the attacks. One of their better players would start skating at top speed cutting in and out of the group as they looked to score quickly. To their surprise I kept pace with him and he never once got the puck. This frustrated them a lot. I did manage to pick off a few passes and start some odd man rushes. I zipped an outlet pass to the forward and he took off like a shot. The other forward also joined on the attack. I got tangled up with one of the other team's players but managed to break free and join the attack as well. They passed back and forth between each other and scored but ignored me. This continued for the rest of the time I played with them.

One day, I recognized one of the guys who was playing. We worked together at Lowe's. We started to talk and ended up on the same team. Thank goodness he was there; he would at least pass me the puck in the offensive zone. I still needed to work on my shot. I really couldn't get much elevation on any shot. He continued to encourage me to keep shooting. Most of the other guys on our team would just take off and play keep away from us. During the game, I took off at top speed from one end of the rink to chase down a puck one of the guys had launched down into the offensive zone. I had a clear path to it. It hit the end board and went behind the net. I tried to turn but didn't make it in time. I crashed into the boards with a thunderous crash. I bounced off the boards and fell to the ice on my back. The boards were shaking because I had hit them so hard. People that worked at the rink counter came into the rink to see what happened. I struggled to get to my feet and barely managed to get back to the bench. I climbed the rail and sat down. Some of the guys asked if I was OK. I slouched over and said yes. My head was throbbing with my helmet on. We had extra people there so there were substitutions.  It came up for my turn and I told one of the guys to take my shift. I needed to set out for several minutes to recoup. I went back out after about ten minutes. I was not as effective as I was earlier. I took some time away from playing to make sure I had a full recovery. I probably had a severe concussion but I never went to the doctor to get checked out.  I continued to skate while I lived in Columbus and picked it up again after I had to move back to Pennsylvania; I still skate to this day. I have never played in a Rec league, but still plan on getting back into playing shape and pursuing this dream.

GOE

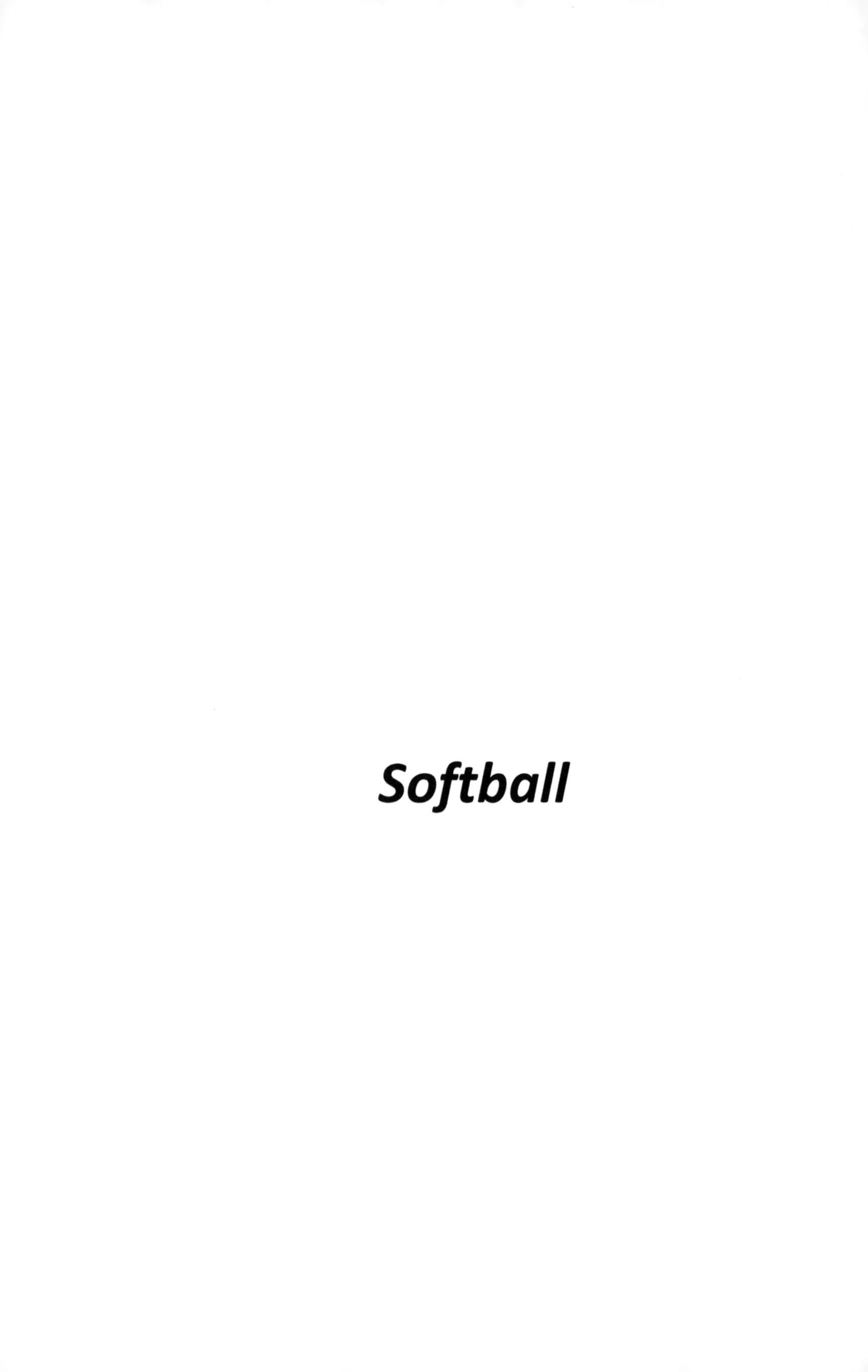

# Softball

I started playing softball when I lived in Ohio. I played on many teams but will focus on the Sand Gnats. This is a team that was comprised of my friends Jimmy, Joe, Judah, several of my lesbian friends and me. We played several seasons together. I usually played shortstop while Jimmy played third and Joe and Judah would pitch or play first base. This was when I met Joe and Judah along with a few other friends that I still stay in contact with. We played in the Sports Monster Recreation Sports League. (My memory is a little clouded due to the medication I used to take. Some of the seasons and chronology might be off.).

During our first season together, we did not do too badly. We won several games and would go out to party afterwards. However, not all the team would go out; it was mostly Jimmy, Joe, Judah, and me. We were a talented team. Everyone played their hearts out. We would always encourage each other to strive to be better. There were also a few other people on the team that first season that I don't remember that well. I remember Jimmy's friend Tracey was on the team along with a young girl named Alyssa. There was also a couple of other guys named Tom and Tommy that graduated from The Ohio State University. Some of these guys would eventually join Jimmy, Joe, Judah, and me on a Sports Monster bowling team after softball season. During one of the games, I was up to bat. I ripped a shot out to right-center. I took off at top speed and rounded the bases before the ball even made into the infield. Tracey looked at me and said, "You really don't need to run that fast." I looked at her and said, "I always play at 100% top speed in every sport I play." She looked back at me and didn't say anything.

The second season we were together, you could see that the team chemistry had greatly improved. Everyone was more comfortable with each other and everyone was assigned a regular position. I still played shortstop, Jimmy played third, and Joe or Judah would pitch. Tommy had taken over first base duties. T, one of my lesbian friends would play second. We won even more games that year than the previous year. We did not make the playoffs, but we were having a blast. All the guys on the team would go to Gresso's or the local bowling alley in Gahanna. They served food and beer and they also had several arcade games, including Golden Tee, which was a big hit with everyone.

The following season was the start of the dark time in my life. I missed most of the season due to severe anxiety and depression. I didn't want to go out in public. I had also lost a substantial amount of weight. The few times that I did show up, I wasn't nearly as good as I used to be. Some of my teammates were very concerned about me. I believe this particular team was an all-guys team. I would show up at Gresso's occasionally and tried to talk with everyone but I was having a difficult time doing so. Jimmy, Joe, their girlfriends, and I would get together at Goodale Park on Sundays to practice. Of course, we had some mimosas before we played. We would also bring beer with us to the park. We always had fun there. It was my sanctuary that kept my anxiety and depression at bay. This was my last season playing softball in Ohio because I had to move back to Pennsylvania due to health problems.

gresso's

# Golf

I never really understood the fascination with golf until I started to play it. I did not see the point of hitting a ball as hard as you could and then having to chase it. My dad had picked up golf and began playing with some of my uncles and my brother. I started playing about my senior year in high school. I started out buying a driver and going to the driving range in Dillsburg, Pennsylvania. I found it very relaxing and a good stress reliever. Eventually, I bought a set of clubs from the local sporting goods in Carlisle, Pennsylvania. I found a pair of golf shoes at the Nike Outlet in Lancaster, Pennsylvania. There were the Tiger Woods special edition shoes. I would practice in my backyard with some of the irons and hit the ball off the warehouse at the edge of our property. Unfortunately, sometimes the balls would clear the warehouse and land in people's yards. I don't think I ever broke any windows; at least not that I'm aware of.

I started going to Piney Apple Golf Course in Gardners, Pennsylvania. Sometimes I would go twice a week. I would meet my cousin Duaine there a few evenings but would mostly go by myself.  I always walked the course. At first, it was only a nine-hole course but then eventually they turned it into an eighteen-hole course. I started to get pretty good. I enjoyed going there to get away from everything.

I continued to play once I started college at Elizabethtown College. One of my teammates from the volleyball team, Brian, would practice with me on the soccer field. A group of us from Ober A-1 went on a golf outing one day. It was a riot! There were only a couple of us that were decent. Most of the guys were just out there to have fun. They would race the golf carts and run over each other's golf balls. They even tipped one of the carts going around a tight turn. They set it up right before any of the golf course employees noticed. If I remember correctly, there was alcohol involved. This was nothing new for us guys though.

I would still go to the driving range when I attended Messiah College. I only went a few times here and there. I was working, plus going to college full-time. I had very little time for anything else. Once I moved to Columbus, Ohio, I would play about once a week at the Eagle's Point apartment complex or Blacklick Golf Course with Don Knoblet and James Arzadon. As I stated in one of my previous stories, I learned to ice skate on the eighteenth hole of the Blacklick Golf Course. Eventually I became too busy to golf and was doing horrible at since I wasn't playing as often. I ended up selling my golf clubs while I lived there.

I took a long break from golf until I had moved back to Pennsylvania due to health reasons. After being back home a couple of years, I started play at the Annual Golf Outreach at Faith Chapel in Carlisle, Pennsylvania. I would go with my dad, my brother, and my uncle, Dick Arnsberger. We always had fun. I still wasn't very good but I had my moments. My Uncle Dick played all the time and was very good. He would always have his trademark cigar while we played. I attended this for several years but could not attend this year (2022) due to my work schedule.

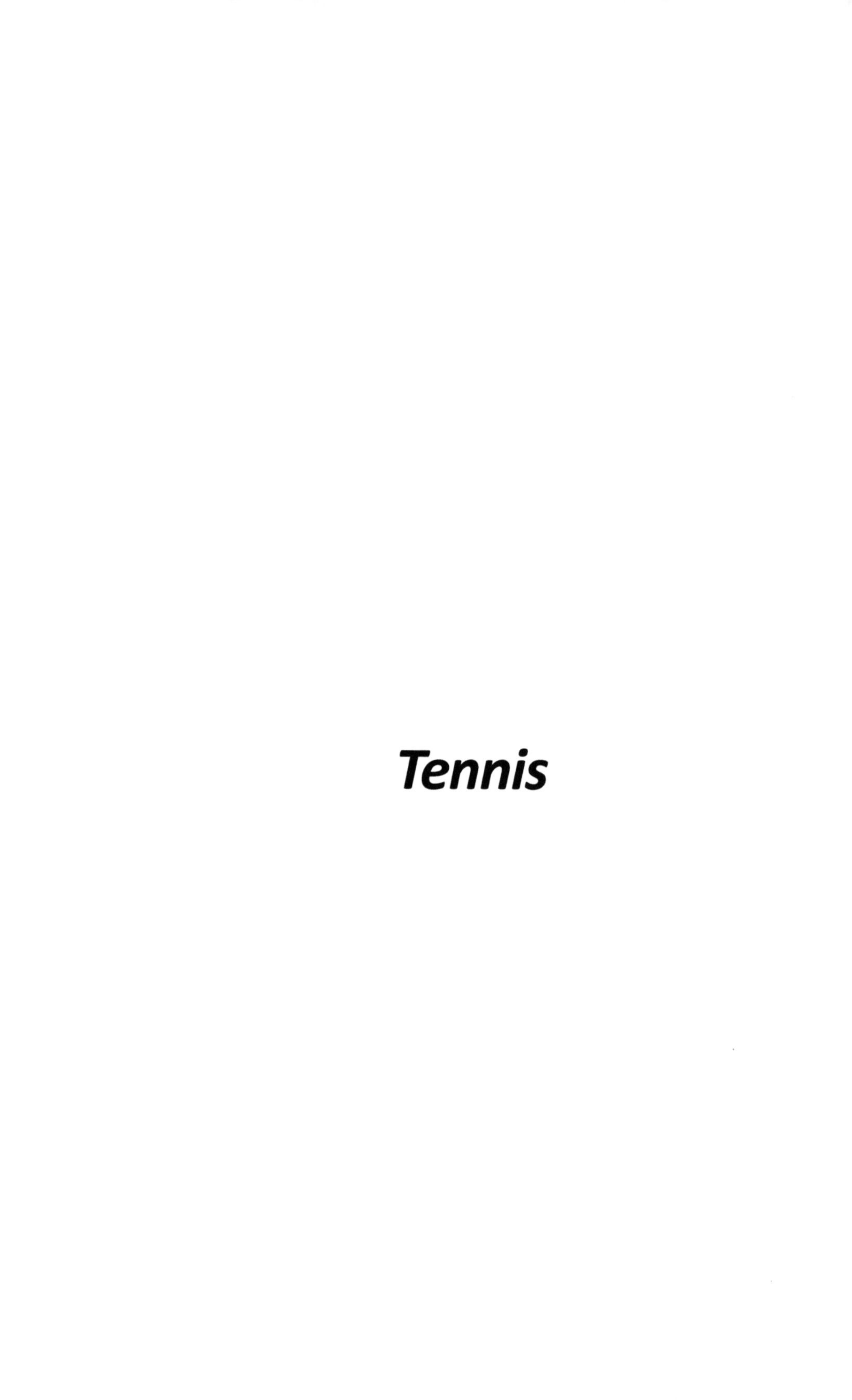

Tennis

I never played tennis competitively, but I decided to add this story so everyone could laugh about my experience. During my time at Elizabethtown College, one of my friends from Ober A-1 told me that one of his friends from high school, who also attended EC, wanted to play tennis with him. My friend had a major exam or project to do and wasn't able to play tennis with her. He asked me if I would play tennis with his high school friend. I said, "Sure. I'm not very good but will give it a shot." She came over to his room and he introduced me to her. He gave me a racket and she and I walked up to the tennis courts. I played horribly; she, however, was really good. She made me look bad on many occasions.  The balls would go flying past me or, when I would return them, I would launch them over the fence with an Andre Agassi style two handed backhand. She laughed uncontrollably. I was to the point that all I could do was laugh along with her.

I didn't play again until I attended Messiah College. I was required to take a racquet sports class for my major. Everyone quickly found out that any type of racquet in my hand equaled bad news. I was horrible. I think I even got worse than when I played that one time at Elizabethtown College.

When I lived in Columbus, Ohio, Don Knoblet was my roommate for a couple of years. We worked together at RentWay, Inc and were both Account Managers. The job was very stressful. When we weren't golfing, we tried to find other things to do to blow off steam. He suggested we start playing tennis. I warned him that I was terrible. A couple of weeks went by, and I decided to buy a tennis racket. I bought a composite racket that was about $60.00. I always tried to buy the best equipment for every sport I played.

One night, after a very stressful week, Don suggested going to The Ohio State University campus and playing tennis on their courts. I was really stressed out and needed to get rid of some pent-up aggression. We got there about 10:30 P.M. or so and the lights were still on and no one was around. "Thank goodness", I said. We started playing. Don had played for several years and, of course, was very good. He ran me all over the court. I didn't return that many shots, but when I did, I hit them over the fence with my two-handed backhand return. This went on for close to thirty minutes. I finally lost my cool and spiked the racquet off the court. It went about fifteen or twenty feet in the air. When it finally landed and I picked it up, the head of the racquet was bowed and bent. This terrified Don. I told him, "Now, I'm ready." He looked sheepishly at me and served. I hit a laser down the line. He was stunned. He kept serving and I was able to return every ball he hit with some authority and accuracy. It was the best tennis I had ever played.

# Billiards

# (Pool)

Billiards is a game of angles and some occasional good luck along with touch. I first took an interest in billiards during my junior year of high school (1991-1992). My friend, Justin and I started going to the local pool halls in Gettysburg and York Springs, Pennsylvania. We would go on the weekends and occasionally one night a week. We did this for several months. Justin and I would mostly play against each other until we were very good. We eventually started playing against other players. We were that good that we would call every shot. We continued to play against other people until some of them wanted to play for money. That is where we drew the line. We worked part-time together at Zeigler Brothers' Feed Mill in Gardners, Pennsylvania while we were in high school. We did not make a lot of money so we thought better of playing for money.

I decided to buy a pool stick and case since we were playing so often. I went to the local K-Mart or Dick's Sporting goods and found one I liked along with a leather case. It was a nice two-piece maple stick. We continued to play all that summer and into our senior year of high school (1992-1993). We always had so much fun.

I took my pool stick with me to Elizabethtown College. I would play an evening or two a week in my dorm with my some of my friends there including Tiny and a few other guys from OberA-1. We had a blast; sometimes we would sneak drinks into the lounge where the pool table was located. We never got in any trouble for that because we never caused any trouble or damaged anything. I ended taking a long hiatus from playing due to working so much along with schoolwork.

I started playing again a couple of years ago once I started working at Home Depot in Carlisle, PA. There was a group of us that starting to go to Three Pines Tavern in Mount Holly Springs, Pennsylvania. Our group would contain about twelve or more people every time.  We would also go to Adam and Sky's apartment complex to play in their community building. I brought my old stick out of retirement. I was very rusty, but soon got back to my old form. Everyone was getting really good. We would call every shot and were even doing trick shots. The craziest shot I have ever while playing pool happened one night at Adam and Sky's. Adam, Sky, and me along with a few other people were playing. It was Adam's turn to shoot. He called the corner pocket. He hit the cue ball and it started spinning, went onto the rail, passed a couple of balls and then hit his ball into the corner pocket. Everyone was like, "How did you do that?!" He looked at us and said, "I don't know; I guess I'm just really good."

I was really into it this time. I had bought a Rigid thirty-six-inch wood lathe and was considering turning pool cues. I am frequent shopper on Ebay and was looking for a piece of lumber to buy. I decided to make a cue out of Koa, a species of wood that is only native to Hawaii. I found the perfect piece, bought it, and had it shipped from Hawaii to my house. I did some more research on how to make a pool cue and purchased the necessary hardware and other components to complete the cue. Once it was finished, I took it to Adam and Sky's place to christen it. It was amazing to play with. Everyone loved it, especially Sky. She was the first person to use it after me. I eventually made a second cue out of reclaimed chestnut. I also took this to Adam and Sky's place to test it out. Everyone was amazed at how well made the cues were. We continued meeting at their apartment complex since Three Pines had shut down due to Covid. Unfortunately, Three Pines opted not to bring back their pool tables once they were reopened. The owners had remodeled the interior and put more dining tables in the restaurant instead of the pool tables. We still get together to play, just not near as often as we would like to. I have enclosed a picture of my pool cues that I made. The one on the left is made from solid reclaimed chestnut, while the one on the right is made from solid Koa.

And onto the next………….